JIM THORPE

World's Greatest Athlete

Written by D. L. Birchfield
Illustrated by Cal Nez

MODERN CURRICULUM PRESS

Program Reviewers

Cathy White Eagle, Executive Director
and President of the Board
Eagle Vision Educational Network
Granite Bay, California

Gwen Sebastian Hill, Teacher
Development Trainer
District of Philadelphia
Philadelphia, Pennsylvania

Joan Webkamigad, Education Specialist
Michigan Department of Education
Lansing, Michigan

Jeffrey Hamley, Director
Native American Program
Harvard University
Cambridge, Massachusetts

Paulette Molin, Ph.D., Assistant Dean
The Graduate College
Hampton University
Hampton, Virginia

Executive Editor: Janet Rosenthal
Project Editors: Elizabeth Wojnar
Mark Shelley

MODERN CURRICULUM PRESS

An imprint of Paramount Supplemental Education
250 James Street
Morristown, New Jersey 07960

ISBN 0-8136-5760-1 (Reinforced Binding)   0-8136-5766-0 (Paperback)
Library of Congress Catalog Card Number: 94-077299

3 4 5 6 7 8 9 10 SP 06

Dear Reader,

This is the story of Jim Thorpe. Jim liked to spend his days running, swimming, and climbing. He loved to play sports and games. At night he would be so tired that he would fall right to sleep.

Jim Thorpe's hard work paid off. He grew up to become one of the greatest athletes in the world. Remember Jim Thorpe's success as you work toward your goals.

Your friend,

Don Bischfield

Early in the morning on May 22, 1887, twin boys were born into the Sac and Fox Nation. They were named Jim and Charlie Thorpe.

The two boys lived with their parents in a one-room log cabin. It was built of cottonwood and hickory trees. The cabin stood on land that is now part of the state of Oklahoma.

As young boys, Jim and Charlie spoke the language of the Sac and Fox Nation. Jim's Native American name was Wa-tho-huck, which means Bright Path.

4

When Jim and Charlie were six years old, they went to the Sac and Fox Indian Agency School. There they were taught English, which was hard for them to learn.

Charlie had an easier time at school than Jim did. Jim would often get into trouble. He found it hard to sit in class when he was used to running and playing outside. Several times Jim left school and ran home. Each time he did this, his father would take him right back to school.

After school, Jim and Charlie would run to the forest. The forest was their playground. They jumped over logs and climbed trees. They often played a game called follow the leader. Wherever the leader would go, the other one would follow. They also swam in a nearby river. Together, they would dive and race.

When the twins were nine years old, something terrible happened. Charlie got sick with pneumonia and died. Jim was so sad that for a while he wouldn't run or play.

Then Jim remembered how he and his brother loved to run through the forest together. So, when he felt sad, he would go out and run. Then he felt better.

When Jim was twelve years old, his parents sent him to the Haskell Indian School in Kansas. They hoped that Jim would like this school. The older boys at the school taught him how to play football. Jim knew right away that football would always be one of his favorite games.

11

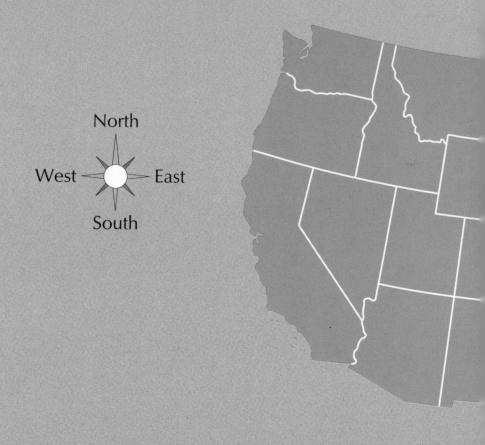

North

West — East

South

When Jim was sixteen years old, he went to the Carlisle Indian Industrial School in Pennsylvania. At Carlisle, Jim could run faster and jump higher than any other boy in school. Jim could also kick a football a very long way.

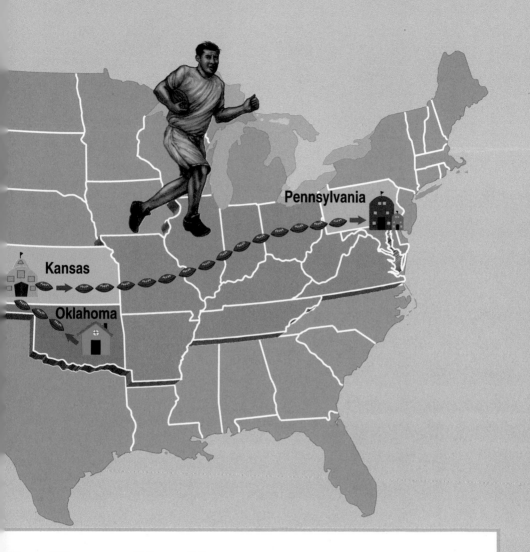

Jim Thorpe Map Key

 - route

 - Birthplace
Prague, Oklahoma 1887

 - Haskell Indian School
Lawrence, Kansas 1899

 - Carlisle Indian Industrial School
Carlisle, Pennsylvania 1904

14

Jim was becoming a great athlete. He broke many records running in races at Carlisle. Jim was a great baseball and basketball player. When he played football, no one could tackle him when he had the ball. Jim also played hockey, swam, wrestled, and boxed. He was always training, practicing, or playing a sport.

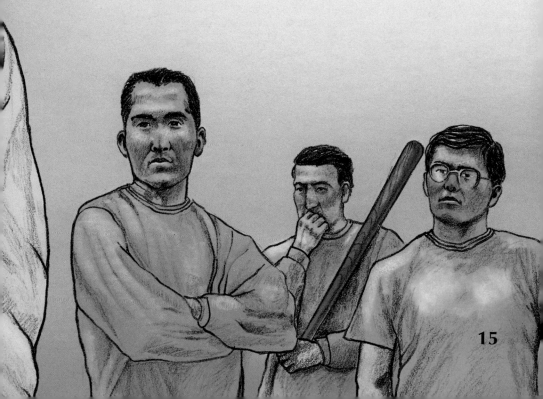

Jim Thorpe

Dwight Eisenhower

Jim even played football against a future president of the United States! In 1912, Carlisle played West Point. Dwight Eisenhower was a West Point student at the time. He later said, "On the football field, there was no one in the world like Jim Thorpe." Carlisle won the game, 27 to 6.

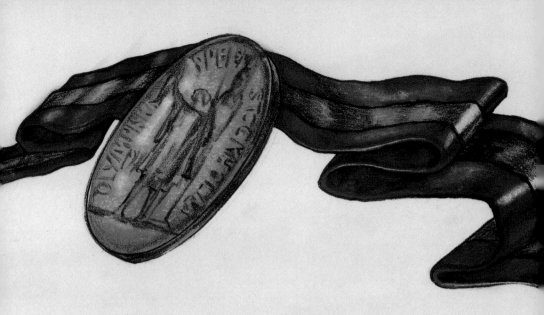

Jim continued to work hard. When he was twenty-four, he went to the Olympic Games in Sweden. He won two gold medals in the pentathlon and the decathlon events. The pentathlon is five events in jumping, running, and throwing. The decathlon is ten events in jumping, running, and throwing. The King of Sweden called Jim "the greatest athlete in the world."

People around the world came to know Jim Thorpe. He played major league baseball and professional football. He became the first president of what is now called the National Football League. Thousands of people started watching professional football just to see Jim play.

23

When Jim was in his early sixties, a movie about his life called "Jim Thorpe—All American" was made in Hollywood, California. This was a happy time for him.

On March 28, 1953, Jim Thorpe died of a heart attack. He was almost sixty-six years old. Today Jim Thorpe is remembered as one of the greatest athletes of all time.

Glossary

All-American (ôl'ə mer'i kən) a title given to a college athlete who is one of the best in the United States

athlete (ath' lēt) a person who is skilled in sports

pneumonia (noo mōn' yə) a sickness of the lungs that makes it hard to breathe

professional (prō fesh'ə nəl) an activity that is done by skilled people who are paid to do it

tackle (tak' əl) to bring a person to the ground

About the Author

D. L. Birchfield is an enrolled member of the Choctaw Nation of Oklahoma. He has a law degree from the University of Oklahoma and is a student of Native American history. Mr. Birchfield believes that it is important that children get accurate and authentic information about Native American cultures and leaders. He is currently working on a book and a play for children.

About the Illustrator

Calvin (Cal) Nez is a native of New Mexico and a member of the Navajo Nation. He was raised in New Mexico by his grandparents who lived the traditional Navajo way. Cal studied illustration at Utah State University, and graphic design at the University of Utah. In *Jim Thorpe,* Cal used prismacolor pencils and airbrush to create a realistic style.